Garden of a Wilted Soul

Crystal Vicci

BookLeaf Publishing

India | USA | UK

Presentation by *BookLeaf Publishing*

Web: www.bookleafpub.com

E-mail: info@bookleafpub.com

ISBN: 9789363319912

First edition 2024

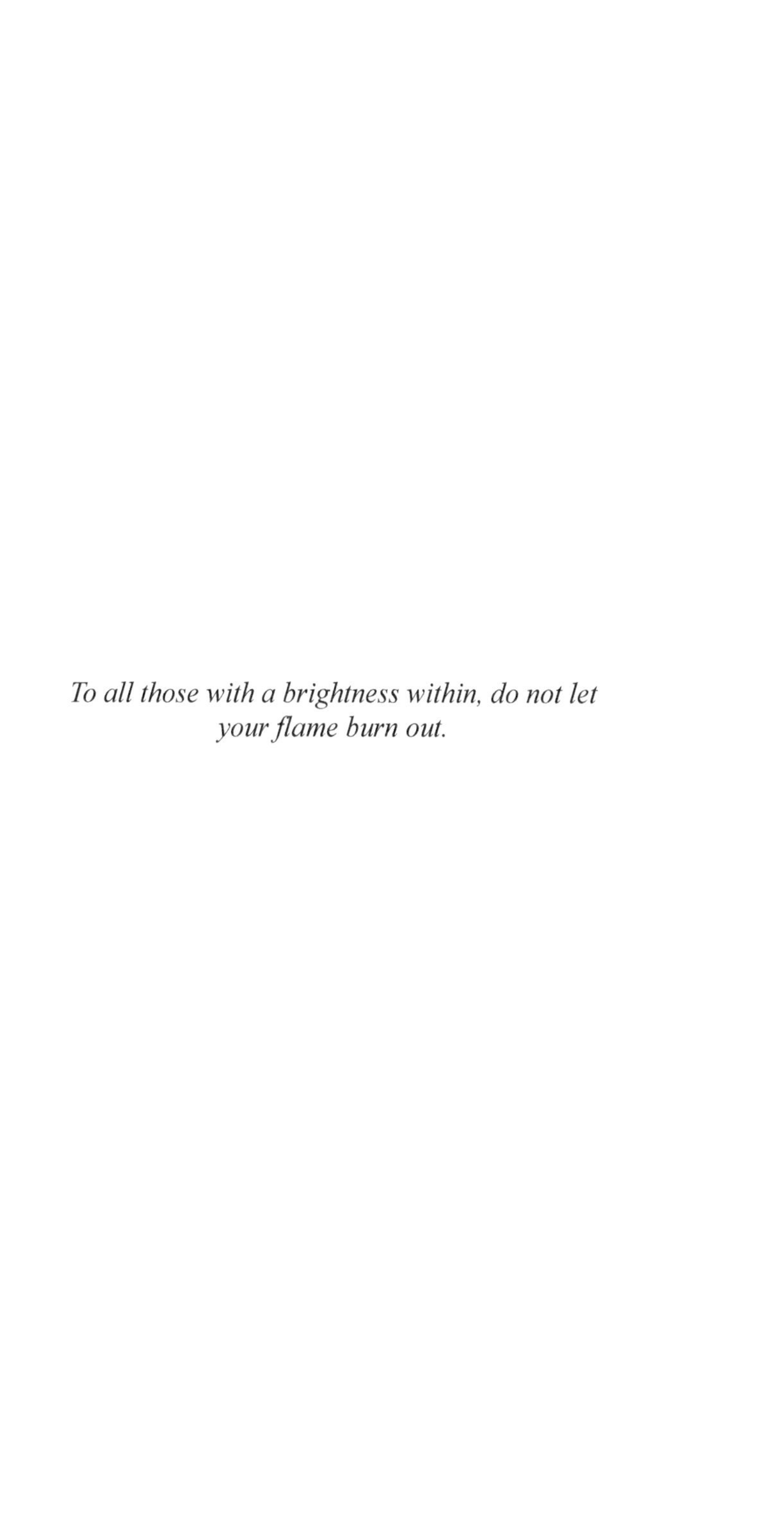

To all those with a brightness within, do not let your flame burn out.

ACKNOWLEDGEMENT

Thank you to all who've been in my life, past and present. My experiences with each of you have shaped me into the person I am, from the smallest subtlety to the biggest influence. I'm forever grateful for the memories I continue to cherish, and more so the lessons I continue to learn. Thank you for allowing me to linger in your lifetimes, even if only for a moment in time.

And a special thank you to Casey – there are no words despite the many I could write to properly describe my thankfulness to have you in my life. You've inspired me to fully embrace who I am again, unapologetically, within this collection and in life. I am forever grateful and appreciative of having met you that day.

One Day

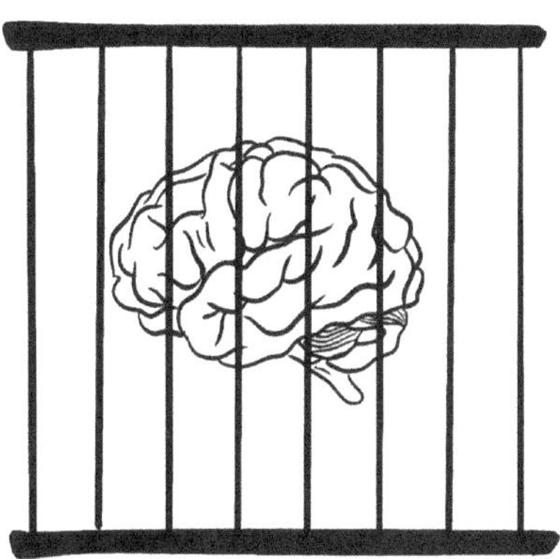

one day i will wake up and not spiral
my tears will be from joy and happiness
my Trauma, past and present, will not control
my thoughts
one day i won't Fear my purpose in life
no longer shy away from the lack of a
Predestined path
and welcome instead the unknown with open
arms

one day i'll feel at peace with the simplicity of
life
the Trivial occurrences of everyday existence
i'll smile at fond memories of former bliss
the Loves i've had, and those i've Lost

one day i'll appreciate the necessity of learning
such Lessons
and Forgive my younger self for how hard she
fought against them
I'll be thankful for the Loneliness that made me
cherish life and love
all the Beauty I'm so grateful to see and live
through

one day I'll say life is Good and I'm okay
and I'll truly Believe it
One Day

But today is not that day

Escape

It's tempting to numb the pain however possible

I want to be past this in my life
The struggle to harm the body I occupy
Just to refocus the anguish in my head
The heaviness of my heart

Would pills put me to sleep for long enough,
chasing away the devastation?
Would a sharp object against my skin help the
tears dry temporarily?

Can the alcohol silence my mind, all the
negativity that seeps in?
Or would something stronger give me the peace
I've longed for?

Is it only in death there is reprieve
Or is death but a gateway to becoming a lost
soul
Endlessly wandering, lonely and broken, stuck
for an eternity
All I wanted was an escape

Compromise

Hopeful bliss—a wondrous outlook on life
Childish eyes taking in the world
Too pure in her gaze, her understanding naive
No fear and ever eager with a gleam in her smile

The first lesson appears—frustration of her
antics
From her safety—a parent, a friend, and family
Maybe if she settles down they'll be less angry
The free-spiritedness must dim

The second lesson stronger—annoyance in her
presence
Her existence is undesired even in innocence
Take less space and fold inward, she'll be wanted

Soften her expressions and speak less of
passions

A third lesson so young—her uniqueness is
wrong
Conform to those around her or be the outcast
Blend in and satisfy the needs of others
Hide herself or be alone, she's not special

The hardest lesson thus far—love
Always treated less than she deserves (so they
say)
Reduce down to the ideal, please them and
maybe
Maybe one day she'll receive the right love

And so it continues, lesson after lesson
Each a reflection of a previous she didn't learn
well enough
More painful and a deeper cut to the soul
Optimizing her confusion in an ever-changing
compromise of who she is

Second Choice

I'm tired of being an option when I'm so much
more
I'm not a second choice
I'm not "just good enough"
My love is one of a kind because I am one of a
kind
But I may be the only one who sees it
Through my glasses shaded by flowers

Panic Attack

Crippling in my own body, my mind takes hold
I attempt a breath that my ribcage refuses
The air entering barely enough to keep me
conscious
I try again while the panic envelopes me
I'm confused and reeling to understand
How could this be right and when does it end
Breathe and focus, stay awake
Sweat drips down, my hair damp
I'm consumed by fear and adrenaline
There's nowhere to go while frozen in place
My mind wanders as my body collapses
Feeling weak as it all comes to an end
I am not safe here but cannot leave
Physically I've survived, mentally I'm scarred

A reminder throughout daily life like a burden
Riddled with shame but nonetheless hopeful to
forget

Soon this will no longer affect me
I am safe

"Friend"-zoned

Words have so much power
Was it truly a joke or a verbalized repressed
thought
Am I wanted here or only tolerated
On a pedestal waiting to be fucked

Am I a distraction from loneliness
Your temporary fixation until life improves
How true and deep do emotions run with
resentment
Do you call me a friend or a challenge

Apology

I'm sorry
For disappointing you, never being brave,
always getting it wrong

I'm sorry I wasn't strong enough
To protect your heart when you were so young,
for not having the courage to stand my ground
and deny the hurtful words said

I'm sorry I let you disappear for so long
Hid you away from the light

It was only to protect you but caused more harm,
you deserved so much more than I could ever
give

I'm sorry for always giving away too much love
Being so consumed with a desire to belong that I
forget you, the damage has been done
Healing can only repair so much

I'm sorry, sweet girl
I'm so deeply sorry for failing you repeatedly
I hope in the final moments that I've fixed things
as best I could
Please forgive my sweet girl; I'll do better in our
next life

You deserved so much better than me, my inner
child

Exhaustion

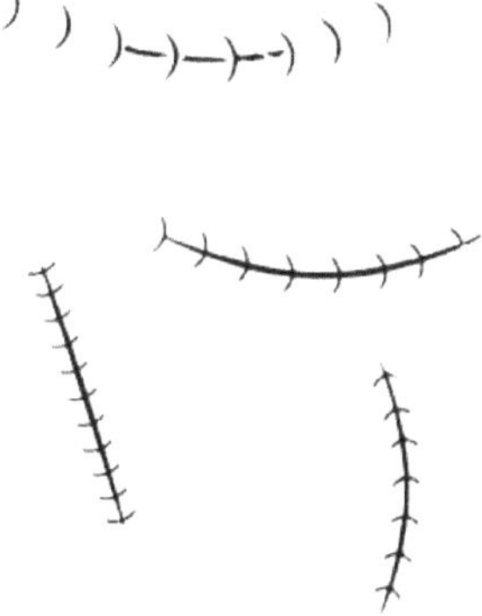

I'm tired of feelings and emotions
Never good enough and only just an option
A second choice that always "deserves better"

I'm tired of desperately craving a love that loves
me
Wholeheartedly and unapologetically
But not worth the effort to reciprocate much

I don't expect or demand a fairytale
I'm loyal to a fault, love the way I long to be
loved
So why does it elude me so

Why are words never followed by actions,
promises always lost and forgotten
But only for me, never for others

I'm tired
When will my heart, mind, and soul accept that
love is not meant for me

When can I rest again for a brief moment of
peaceful numbness
And then try again in another life
Where maybe, just maybe, I'll finally be
worthwhile

Ever Searching

I search for you
for your affection
for your attention
for your admiration
for your unconditional love

I search for you
in the small gestures
in the messages that are more than just words
in the effort to make distance seem small

I search for you
the compassion and consideration

the desire to show interest in my interests
the willingness to do things even when it's not
your preference
the drive to see me happy and feeling safe and
loved

I search for you
Longingly
Hoping that once I've found you, you'll be mine
to keep instead of a lesson to learn

Keep

Break me a little
Then break me more
Keep chipping away until there's nothing left
Because maybe then I'll really know what I hold
My worth and purpose

So keep breaking me
Find out if one day I won't fight back
If one day I'll finally crumble into nothingness
Hollow and shattered
Keep trying to break me

Because I never will

Dear Friend

Hello, nice to meet you, known stranger
Not sure where you've been all this time
Let's get to know each other again, been a while

How about a drive while we share music
An enthusiastic discussion of our passions
Come over and waste time laughing
Share secrets and dreams in our little world

I wish I knew why fate took so long
And silently plea you'll stay longer this time
The memories, the adventures, the inside jokes
Let's build an endless collection of moments

Despite whatever ending we'll endure
I'm grateful for having known you, my friend

Sea Breeze

She peers through a window as her eyes glaze
over
Already lost in a daydream of momentary bliss

Wind whipping through her hair
While she smells the sea in the breeze
A sunset just beyond the horizon
Softens her face to a light pink while her eyes

Her eyes reflect the light within
A fiery blood orange

Darling

I miss the innocence of my youth
The young girl who thought the hardest part of
life was commercials
The little girl who believed her ninja turtles
would keep her safe
Against all monsters, real and imaginary
The naive one who stayed hopeful for that one
person
One person to know her, understand her, accept
her in all faults
So small and sweet in a world so complicated
My darling if only you knew what life held for
you

You'll have to stay strong at every turn, every
aspect
From those who hurt you in more ways than one
Those who made you feel alert instead of safe
Who took for their needs, who never gave
Sweetest babe you may feel that breathing is a
struggle
Never fully at ease with others or within
yourself
You may never be seen and remain an enigma
Please understand it's only for this lifetime
Stay strong to make it through, have courage
And then my dear you can rest and heal
I know it's hard and will continue to be
And you'll want to escape, to let go
But little one, there's only one of you
Don't burn out just yet
Just to spite them and break the cycle
Don't let your flame die

Blue

Like a moth to the dancing flicker of a flame
Burning low with a glowing blue I lingered
toward the danger
Will I turn to ash, betrayed by its beautiful
whimsy
Or will I be surrounded by soft warmth

Detached Illusions

Is love timeless
Detached from perceptions
Oblivious to outside influences

When is it worth fighting for
How does one determine the depth involved
Do you willingly sink while trying to swim

Too

How hopeful is too hopeful
Unrealistic versus optimistic
Blind ignorance instead of delusion

Silence

The silence can be deafening
And yet elegantly peaceful

But only if my mind remains quiet too

Little Circle

Having girlfriends is such a privilege
Having friends at all is a privilege
It must be a beautiful experience
To have a network of people who care for you
Outside of family and lovers
Being accepted and wanted for company
To share memories with
Have someone to talk with

Sometimes I can't help but wonder
What's it like to belong in my own little group

Choices

What is love?

Is it the subtle touch as you walk past them in
the kitchen
The look you give when you know they won't
admit they want to try your food despite having
their own
A gentle kiss to the forehead at the end of a long
day
Whispered "I love you" around company to
preserve an intimate moment only you share
The gentle caress while looking deeply into each
other's eyes
"I made you this"—a meal, poem, favorite drink
"I thought of you today and had to share"—an
experience, a material object, an inside joke
The most trivial of things, one small gesture

Listening to something of interest that's not your
own
Comfort during a hard moment in the mental
battle we all encounter
Confirmation and consideration, transparency
A safe home ready to battle any obstacle to
make this last
Ongoing efforts to combat complacency
A willingness to learn how to love the person
The one you CHOSE to be with because of your
connection

Companion

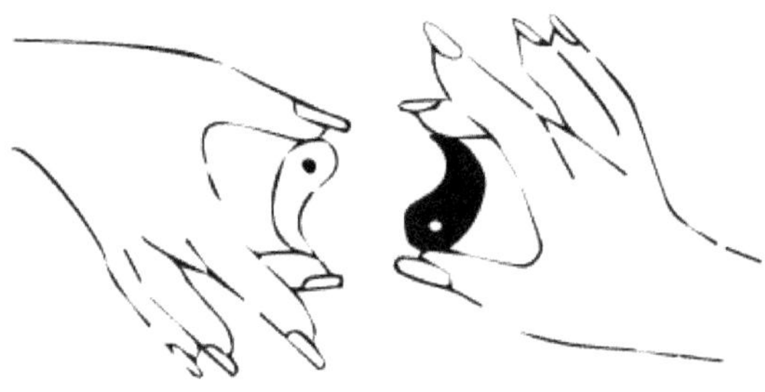

The moon, it shines so brightly
Calling to her wolf
Out of reach yet connected

The cycles she's bound to
A fate not desired but bestowed upon
She must start anew so frequently

The wolf watching always for a glimpse
Waiting timelessly to howl his love for her
For the brief moments of solace they share

She longs to be close, destroy the distance
He longs for her to stay, full and shining
brilliantly
But she departs and he must too

Their fates intertwined and yet cruel
A kismet path of longing
Requited love at its finest and most endearing

Travel on the Wind

The sun graces my face with warmth
The clouds scarce in the blue above me
I sit and enjoy the beauty around

The wind comes at night in a gust
The stars dancing beside the moon
I'm shaken to my core and it's my time to travel
To move forward and leave my home of comfort

I'm carried far, not staying in one place for long
Until I arrive to rest amongst a soft landing
The morning dew glistening around the delicate
blades

I am content here
I shall change soon
Until it's my time to sleep
And be reborn on my branch once again

Maybe

Could it be true
That what I manifest comes to light
What I've wanted will be fulfilled
Or is it momentary bliss

Do I get excited or stay neutral
Hopeful that the universe will finally
Finally give me what I've worked for
What I deserve in blessings

Revery

Green fields covered in flowing grass
Light kisses to bare ankles
Her yellow skirt dancing in the breeze
A painted sky enraptures overhead
Purples, pinks, oranges cast by the setting sun
Clouds dusting the rays, whispering a goodnight
The flowers consuming the senses
Soft melodies from the animals settling
Nature surrounding, ignorant of the world
A calm lake just beyond the fields
Ready to sparkle with the stars
A deep breath and all is calm
Serene but a fleeting moment amid the chaos

Ablaze

Come close and whisper soft
Let your lips grace my cheek
A smile so delicately given
Your hand caressing my neck
Kiss me with a gentleness
An intensity starts to build
Your hands wandering
Eyes ablaze with longing
Nestle into me with need
Our bodies becoming one
Intertwined with heavy breath
A rushed desire to be connected
Our physical forms bringing to life
What our hearts already know
A love of acceptance and safety
An abundance of heated passion

A Dance

You crossed my path unexpectedly
Hearing my earlier petition
Was it a rendezvous of fates intertwining
My soul recognizing yours and I knew we'd fall
in course
Bound through music, pain, growth
Healing my broken pieces and finding myself
again
While you learned to let the past go gently

So in love and yet not chosen
By the one you want that always questions
A game of cat and mouse dredged in affection
Will I win gracefully or die from desertion

Is it realistic or are we insane
For you to bend the knee and I take your name

A life together all the same
Or will overthinking and fear be to blame
For if we're jaded we'll surely fade to nothing
But the love, the memories will forever remain

Am I

I want love but I now realize I don't know what
love is
I know what it means when I apply love to
others
But in receiving it I am clueless

I love in the subtleties and gestures
I announce it openly and express in a number of
ways
I can be romantic, sexual, compassionate, gentle,
respectful
I won't yell when we're at each other's throats
I won't say things I don't mean out of high
emotion

I treat us as a whole and not separate when faced
with hardship
I can be understanding even in moments when I
don't understand
Is it wrong to want the same treatment
For someone to acknowledge that trivial stuff
matters
And then show they understand me
To experience love languages the way I express
for others
Is it my own downfall to desire a reflection of
my love
Are my wants and more importantly, my needs a
delusion I've ignored for so long
Am I now living a fantasy with reality fighting
against my spirit
Am I broken beyond repair when it comes to
feeling loved

Am I truly alone in life like I've been told

Pure Reaction

Laughter is an amazing remedy
Such a pure reaction to bubble up from within
The joy behind someone's eyes as they bellow
out
Slap of the knee and tears of happiness

Regardless of what you're going through
The hardships fall away
A temporary relief
Releasing the stress and relaxing the shoulders

Find the fun in life and laugh
A subtle giggle or full-blown hysterics
Let the joy exist with a smile in your eyes
And a gentleness on your breath

Let go and laugh from your heart

Haze

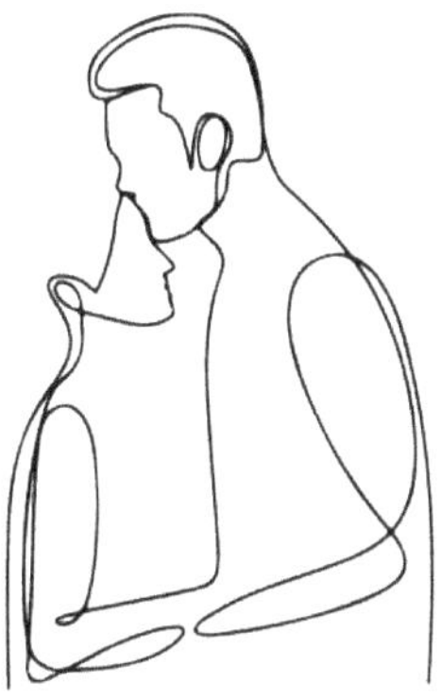

I let you in to crumble all my walls
Showed the deepest parts of me
All the cracks and broken foundation
The flaws and lows I had clung to

You saw it all and braved the fall
Into a love so unconditional
Accepted me despite my wounds
Gave a light to follow just beyond the haze I was
held under

Your smile and patience, acceptance
A sense of security and wanting
Was a long road to take, a slow love begins

Through rough patches and hardships
The emotional trials and healing spirals

We brought each other out of the darkness
I reached my hand out to you
The fear crippling but the flame burning bright

We'll fight like hell before we give in
Before we let this love falter
A story written in time and what an adventure

Happy Squeak

"I missed you"

You called because you missed me
I was on your mind
My heart fluttered at the words

"Say it again" just to savor the sweetness

"I missed you babe"

I smiled so widely a squeak escaped me
To know I'm longed for
To discover it is mutual and I'm not only
fantasizing
My heart skips and the oxytocin rushes
I feel giddy
I feel in love like it's still the first day
Like we're still at the festival
Enjoying the spark surrounding us

Distant

Off the distant shore I search for something
more
More meaning
More to life
More of who I find myself to be

Love
Laughter
Peace

Off the distant shore I think I've found the more
I've been longing so long for
A purpose
A craving
Safety for who I've become

A home

But now on the distant shore I need one thing
more to enjoy endlessly what I've captured
Time

Hopeful Idea

I hope we were more than fleeting
We have more opportunities to explore together
As best friends and even more—partners

I crave the closeness I feel with you
The warmth felt in your arms
Slowly falling asleep to your heartbeat
Whispered thoughts as we drift

The plans we could make, ideas we have
I wish the universe gave us a better start
Less distance and healed spirits

Have strength to brave the challenges
Endure the struggles only to come out stronger

My Affections

I show my affections and true feelings in every
aspect I can
"Be safe"
"I miss you and wish you were here"
"Want to do another movie night"
"Can I see you again"
"Let's do something together"
"I love you"
"Ramble to me because I love listening to you"
"It's a lovely thought for one day"
I want to add to your life while you add to mine
I care for you on a level no words can describe
The love unconditional without judgement or
prejudice
Connection so deep I knew before I even saw
your face

It's scary and unbelievable at times
Something so RARE it makes you question its
validity
But remember it can be real despite what your
mind understands
Traumas telling you it's fake
Obstacles trying us at every turn
Yes we are challenged repeatedly
To make sure we are ready for the depths
involved
But it can be real
It can be happy without "an ending"

Pathway

Uncertainty
It can kill dreams
Possibilities that were limitless
Turned to ash in an instant
Decisions changing timelines in a blink of an
eye
One version on a path of love and another
Endlessly grieving the course
The what-ifs frustratingly infatuating
Continuously burned
Singed at the edges of my heart
Cracks added to my mental state
Remembrance of another time
Another lesson

Restless Again

Another restless night in my lonely bed
Watching the lights dance across my ceiling
In shades of the sea from the North
Stars sparkling like bioluminescence
I toss and turn with only discomfort to greet me
My eyes heavy but rest does not come
What caused this awakened tiredness
Keeping me tethered to the conscious world
What stops me from falling into a dreamland I
wish to enjoy
Is it the blankets not keeping me safely tucked in
The stuffed animals on either side providing a
temporary closeness
Is it my sensitive hearing
Picking up the slightest sound beyond the walls I
am surrounded by

I only long to have a moment in my
subconscious
To spend with the one I want so desperately by
my side
Is that not reason enough for my mind to quiet
My body to still in deep breath
If only for a moment until reality returns again

Uphill

Life... it's fucking hard
I'm exhausted and defeated
Growth always seems to be greener on the other
side of that mountain
No one tells you it's for a higher self that you'll
never meet
Hope that self is doing better in the end

Persistence

Did I push too hard to warrant a sadness
Did my persistence destroy your smile
Have my efforts been overwhelming
Is there no option to reconcile

I wanted so badly, craved the abundance
Over my head without an understanding
The impact so heavy it came down like a blade
Cut us apart, two hearts disengaging

My presence a mere agitation

Discovered

I learned a lesson, took a few tries
I was good enough, that much was clear,
I've always been good enough
Standing here alone attempting to mend mind
and soul from the dance held
I helped you heal and grow all the while I
learned self-love is a kindness

I'm grateful for the moments, though I hate the
pain accompanied

The fool

Filled with hopefulness and desperation
Blinded by rose and the sweet nectar of affection
Was it so noble an assumption
That I'd finally found my home

Safety promised for a worthy queen
Armor abundant did little to shield
From the swift strike to the most vulnerable

From Flame to Death

I break down from all the thoughts running
through my mind
The what-ifs and negative self-talk I try to
ignore
What if I'm not good enough and nothing more

Should I not be stronger than this, sitting
teary-eyed
All over a possible reality of me becoming lost
I wasn't well before that wish I made that
musical day
I fear I'll be worse again should he take his
leave one day
But I'd let him come back every time

Teapot

I broke down today
I was a teapot that hit its boiling point and
whistled
Loudly in blistering agony

My thoughts stirred in my gut
Broke through the silence instilled as a cage
I let the tears fall and my heart hurt

I spoke words I dreaded into reality
I battled myself in fear of more pain and
complication
My world came to a head and my mental state
Its fragility cracked from my own doing

I broke
But I still try to remain strong

Haunting

I haunt the places I've been
A trail of my essence remaining
Frozen in time, played on repeat
Infinite versions looping on the planes
Do others sense me
Have the emotions lingered within

I haunt those who've interacted
A phrase, a mannerism, a laugh
The energy transfers and imprints
I follow when they depart
Pieces of my spectrum scattered

Is this what it is to be known
Reminders within the intricacy of life
Randomly impacting the waves of others

Will I ever understand the path I leave behind
How I was seen and what I meant to them
Forever haunted

Melt Away

My head is splitting
Is it my mind causing chaos or only a migraine
I lay in an uncomfortable ache
With my closed eyes conjuring up images
Happy thoughts of love and intimacy
Whatever it thinks will help me feel better

Being held again with a kiss placed on my
forehead
Someone taking care of me because they want to

Rubbing my neck and shoulders to help
Release all the tension
Let the pain go
And melt into the comfort

Slow Down

I need a restful day of peace and sleep
Life can be stressful and confusing
Let my body recover while I daydream

Roulette

How are people chosen for their karma

Those who only receive good regardless of their
actions
Who find wealth or love or get what they most
desire
While others get the hardest trials

If you're always good and try your best
Does it open doors for receiving blessings
Or is it just life

Or is it roulette
And YOU just chose wrong

Break My Heart

I break my own heart

With the hope that you're mine
By wanting more than I deserve
In expectations
Believing in love

I break my heart by holding on too long
Feeling everything
Wishing I was good enough
Inability to move on
Incapable of accepting reality with blind
ignorance

I break my own heart by being me
I want the feelings to end

I want the light to go out
My heart to crack for the last time

Bury The Numb

I feel alone

I'm falling into my abyss of emotional pain
I'm trying desperately not to spiral
Why is it so hard when it used to be so easy
When being numb and ignorant was second
nature

I want to be secure in myself again
No longer needing reassurance constantly
Bury away the feelings and overwhelming
affections
Just BE in this ever-confusing world

Anxiety

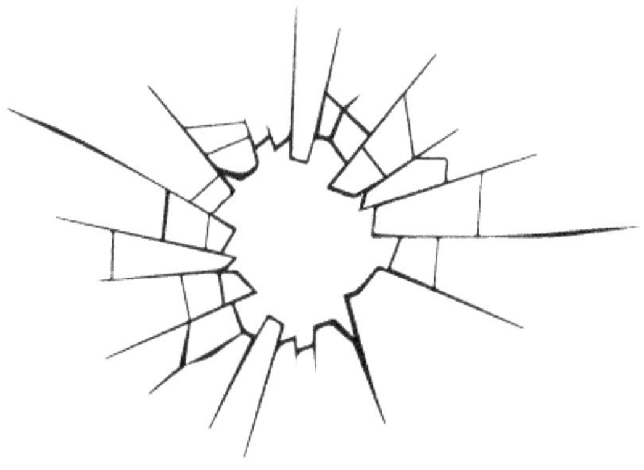

My mind races with the what-ifs
Paralyzing me in a state of apprehension
How do I determine what's paranoia
Versus my intuition with heightened senses
The anxiety of an unknown
Always penetrating my walls so thick
Through the cracks and crevices of my
foundation
I try to let go of the wondering
The thoughts running around
Causing my stomach to drop
Forcing my heart to quicken
I don't want to be like this
Creating false scenarios of worry
Forcing my body into unnecessary ruin
I want to silence the noise
I want to live in the now

I want to feel confident in myself
And in the world that surrounds me
In my life and my peace

Why

Why are you like this
Why are you so broken and damaged
Why can't you figure your shit out
Why can't you heal

Why do you speak this way about yourself

Alone

Let the music flow through your veins
Consuming you for endless hours
You are alone in life, despite your resistance

Despite the fear and loneliness
You will be okay one day

Alignment

I don't belong here
Not in the way of breathlessness though
My spirit craves a peace which doesn't exist
The old soul within this vessel
Glimpses of a past life, emotions I've never lived
Timelines crossed making it difficult to
determine this phase with another
So aligned and yet completely confused
Held so high to an unachievable pedestal
One I didn't ask for and one I can't seem to fall
from

Connections are hard but observance is natural
I'll know more in a glance than I could ever
speak into words
A healer towards others, shared wisdom and
experiences
The skies have a different meaning - the stars,
the moon
It's not the view I desire and miss
The lack of compassion from people
disappointing
Vibrations all wrong and constant tension
Where is it I feel at home and will I know it
again one day

Minor

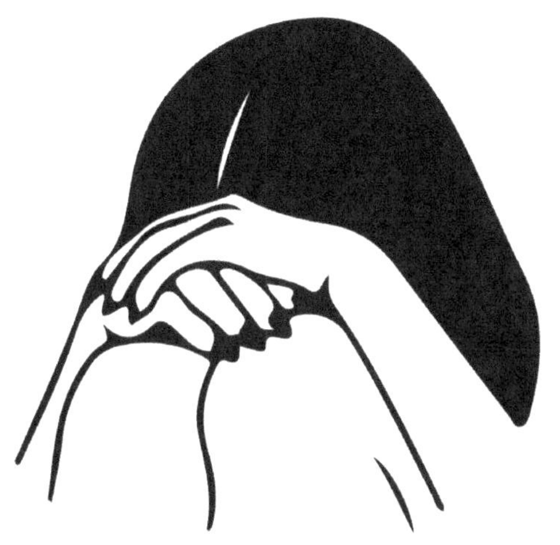

I struggle forward with a goal
For the day I feel content
Fulfilled
To be good even with minor inconvenience

Tower

Gloomy
More than the clouds bellowing overhead
The grey consuming the light of day
Timid tears falling from the skies and cheek

My heart and world reflecting the sorrow within
A regret and a loss
The tower I fought to keep standing with a dying
passion
Crumbled to dust
The fire struggling for one last breath

Come back to me
Let us rebuild

Do it

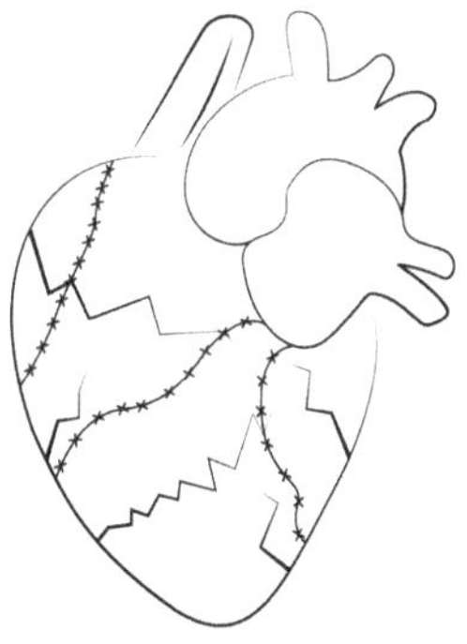

It can be done
Healing
Overcoming
Courage and conviction
It's a hell of a process
Difficult and painful at times

But if you can withstand the challenges
And come out victorious
Even if bruised
You've done it
Be proud of your accomplishments
No matter how trivial to another
They are yours
Be thankful for your strength
Acknowledge yourself with love

Melodic

To be surrounded by sound
How do you describe such unity
All voices as one in solid melody
Abundantly synchronous and individual
To share such passion and love of a
commonality

A unity of quintessence encircled by the hum of
breath

Down the Road

Traveling a road of memories
Emotions flowing on the breeze
We walk to the past to appreciate the present

What could I have become
Shown what's not seen before
And influenced under a different sky
Gifted with the wisdom of a lifetime spent

Who I should've been, faded away
The possibilities gone from view
How do I continue with what I've learned
While creating new moments in realignment

Lingering Remnants

I wonder what you think of me
Do I linger on your mind easily
When you see something that would've made
me smile
Or hear a phrase I would've laughed at
abundantly
How do I cross your thoughts
Does it hit you like a freight train at full speed
Or is it so subtle for you to brush off in lieu of
better things

Does an invisible thread remain woven to me
Do you dream of me
Do you lie awake and remember I'm not there
with longing in your heart

Do you wonder about me
Where I am and how I've healed
Do you wish for one more moment

Who was I to you
Will I ever know or do I only have my thoughts
My fantasies and delusions
Is it my own self-projection which stares back at
me
That you feel for me as I do for you because it's
easier to accept than reality

Here

I wish you were here
To experience life with me

The joy of a concert running through your body
The peace of sitting in a rose garden with the
sun beaming
Relaxing at home watching a movie or reading a
book
Watching each other exist together while
maintaining individuality

Let's go for a walk surrounded by the fall leaves
Sit together drinking hot chocolate by the
fireplace
The snow falling like fluffy stars just beyond the
windows

Listening to our records figuring out who wins
the selection
Making cookies while flirting in the kitchen

I wish you were here with me
To stargaze at night and make a wish
Lean on each other in the tough moments
And laugh in unison during our goofy times
Adventures in every facet regardless of cost
Having a life together built of memories and
love

I wish you were here with me
In love with me and ready to take on our world
Together

Maybe one day

Temperance

A revelation fell upon my mind
The lack of coincidence in life
Release what isn't controlled
And suddenly all starts falling
Into the places I long to be
Flowing in honeyed revery
Blissfully aware of the pace
Bestowed upon my senses
I wait in earnest and patience

Self Reflection

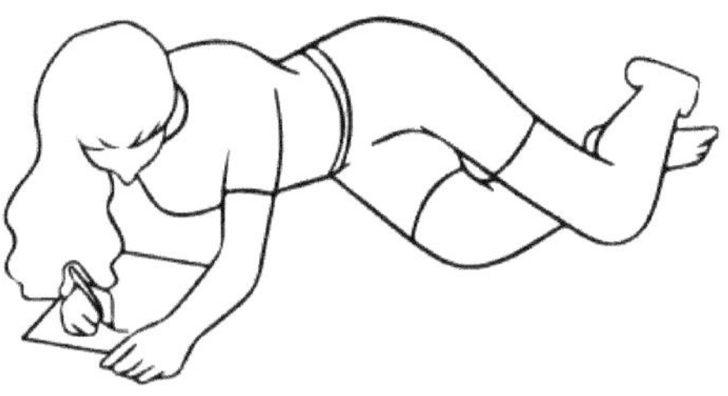

I sit and stare at the wall
Pondering on thoughts that cross my path
A fleeting memory of my inner child laughing
Another as a teenage overwhelmed with toxicity
I reflect on a friendship gone silent
How I played part in the history I helped write
Questioning what decisions I made in error
Which ones a blessing disguised as loss
Fearful for my future to become better
Willing to learn and grow
My past a reminder of where I've been
My future unknown and barely controlled
My present confusing but ongoing
I dream to be peaceful and fulfilled
Still determining how to accept the harsh
realities
Allow the emotions to flow and be released
Be grateful for the moments
Understand not everything comes to a happy end
It's okay to be lost and scared

Try your hardest with leniency and grace
And rest if needed
And then move forward again

Caged

I understand the animals at the zoo
Caged in with such little room to roam
Like being locked into a life you didn't ask for
And somehow can't fully escape
My mind is my cage at times
Constantly running about things I can't control
Wondering if I'm finally on the right path
Or aimlessly spinning in circles
Cycle after cycle

Release

The fear you have of being alone
The fleeting desire to be someone
The heartache, the sorrow
The confusion and the longing
The feeling of everything out of your control

Let it go

Breathe darling and let it go
Be grateful for what you have in life

If it was meant for you in how you daydream
It'd already be yours
If you're not worthy or deserving
Then accept and let it go

Amidst a Glow

Sparkling eyes and magical lips
In a soft blue dress so docile
She twirls in joy
A beauty exuding from within
Her confidence coming alive
Once so scarce now glowing
A radiation of bright light
So pure and warm in the darkness

Learning For Me

I'm learning to be grateful for what I have
And accept what's not for me
Learning to let go despite the sadness it might
bring
Smiling at the fond memories that linger
Allowing the bittersweetness to be

It's hard and some days are better than others
Knowing what you wanted
It may not be for you in this life
Acknowledge the losses
Process and heal
And when you're ready
Find the joy in existence again

Missing

I miss you sweet girl
Your unconditional love
The cuddles on the couch
Your comfort during hard times
Being yelled at every time I came home
No matter how long I was gone
Always greeted with that sweet face
Wanting my attention when working
Talking on every recorded meeting
Everyone who knew you misses you
I miss you
Everyday

Balance

I want to live more for me
Live my life to my fulfillment
How do I ensure I'm able to do such
Without hurting others involved

Do I act selfish with no regard
Should I consider others and be cautious
I long for the ability to prioritize myself
While still maintaining what's meant for me

I'm not looking to hurt others in my process
I want to be happy and at peace
And for this I'm at war with myself
To find the balance within

Heal

I hope one day you're able to heal
When love comes you'll be ready to hold it
The past and all the trauma will be washed away
It'll no longer be temporary, you'll be home and
safe

I hope you find happiness—in the little things, in
yourself
That other person you choose is what you need
and want
Become better—*grow*—for you
Don't let it go so easily because of hard
circumstances

You deserve your peace, calm
I hope it finds you

Don't Fear

Don't fear the depths you'll go

You'll reach the abyss of your mind
Pull out every scrap of pain
In search of clarity to move forward
Allow the pain and hurt
The confusion to take hold
Recognize your body is trying to remember
And then release it all
Release and reject it from your soul

Healing can be a torturous process
Full of emotional rollercoasters and chaos
Understand what you've been through
How it's affected you
And then grow from what you've learned along
the way

Let your chest fill with breath
The tears be shed
Vocalize your agony

And then calm yourself
Breathe deeply
Whisper thoughts of peace
And let it go

The painful memories and the trauma of a past
life
They are not your present

The moments have passed
You are safe and you are healed
Grown with strength and new wisdom to endure
You are not HER from your past

You've reached the depths
And you survived to thrive in spite

Give It Time

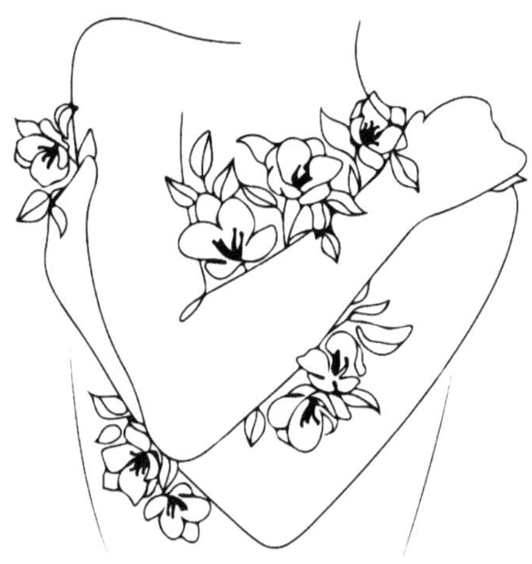

Willpower does overcome
Manifest your happiness
It all starts within and expands outward
You can do all you've wanted

Be strong, the darkness will fade
Give it time
The heartache will heal
Light is coming, you only need to hang on

You've got this

Sweetest Mention

The sweetest of innocent intention
Smallest gestures imprinted with affection
A word sending shivers of safety throughout

Together

I sit and contemplate a world in my mind
Where we are one and love thrives
There's understanding and acceptance
Unconditional in the most subtle of ways
Compersion for each other
We stand together connected
Ready to fulfill the journey, our purpose
We got this

RARE

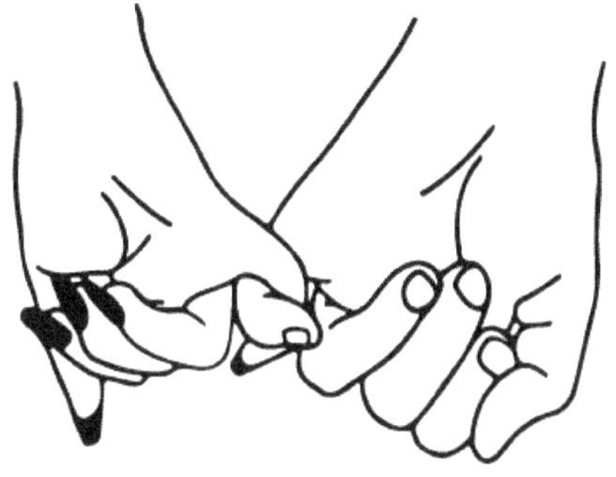

It's rare
It's real and it's ours
Trauma of the past be damned

RARE is worth it

You are worth it

We are worth it

I AM WORTH IT